laundry & LOVE NOTES

laundry & LOVE NOTES
a poetic memoir

———————

ALICIA ZAKON

7AKON
PRODUCTIONS

Laundry & Love Notes
a poetic memoir

Copyright © 2014 by Alicia Zakon

For more information on special discounts for bulk purchases,
please send an email to info@aliciazakon.com

Cover Design & Book Design by Daniela Mejias
Cover Photography by Andrew Bramasco
Illustrations by Marcelo Guiterrez

Library of Congress Control Number: 2013902084

ISBN 978-0-9888646-0-3
10 9 8 7 6 5 4 3 2
Printed by Nize Printing - www.nizeprinting.com

ZAKON
P R O D U C T I O N S

For Tanya, a soft-spoken yet wildly creative young woman who devoted her late-twenties, thirties, and early-forties to raising three vibrant, inquisitive and strong-willed girls. You're boss.

untitled
by my mother, Tanya
Circa 1980 (age 21)

walking down the street
head looking over shoulder
thinking someone must be behind
then quickening your pace when you're sure they're gaining on
you
looking for love
an understanding word
i feel hard like brick
cold like ice

CONTENTS

INTRODUCTION

———————

home is where you do laundry. uproot hamper from corner and unstuff crumpled clothing. judge between light and dark. handwash with elbow grease and linedry for neighbors to see.

on the clothesline, heartache sags like damp winter sweater, sways till it softens. delicate lingerie wave until confident in their beauty, no longer named unmentionable. family woes weigh heavy like wet jeans, stiffen to cardboard when dry. last to leave the line. first to wear outside.

my words are my laundry, written in each place i've called home. inked by lamplight yesteryear and last night. this is my heap of folded secrets. my hamper of love notes. etched with elbow grease and pinned up to catch the breeze. fly free.

from child to woman, this is me.

—————

i am eight years old when my mom moves us from a housing project in Richmond to Berkeley, my sisters are ten and six. a year after we move, my dad assaults my mom. it is the first time that my parents' arguments have escalated to physical violence. i don't see my dad for four years.

with dad gone, my sisters and i bicker with mom. often fights between my mom and older sister are so intense the police are called. at age sixteen, my older sister moves out.

when i am fourteen my dad moves back in with us for a year. by this time, i have built a solid life outside of home. i join a caring but controlling church that demands much of my free time. the remainder is busied with dance, track, and afterschool/summer jobs.

my church thinks we should only date people who share our exact religious beliefs. i agree with the concept, but i don't like anyone in my congregation. so i start secret relationships with guys outside my church and break up with them when it becomes clear they aren't fitting into my life.

If There Was Peace
May 1994 (age 10)

If there was peace
Everyone would agree
Let there be peace
What a difference it would be

If there was peace
No one would commit crimes
If there was peace
No would ask, "Could you spare a dime?"

If there was peace
Everyone would get along
If there was peace
Everyone would be where they belong

If there was peace
No one would kill
If there was peace
Everyone would have enough money to pay their bills

If there was peace
Everyone would have a place to live
If there was peace
People would learn to give

If there was peace
Everyone would be satisfied with who they are
If there was peace
No one would be locked behind bars

If there was peace
If there was peace

running
June 1995 (age 11)

i'm running
running
not from anything
not from anyone
just running

the breeze makes my hair run wild
and i feel like i'm trying to win a race
a race of life
a race of survival

that's how life is

with the wind
June 1995 (age 11)

things will flow with the wind
things will flow right
things will flow the way they're supposed to
right along with the wind

but who knows when the wind will change direction
it's only in destiny's hands
who knows where the wind will lead me
for now i'll flow with the wind

blank
June 1998 (age 14)

as if my eyes were grey rainclouds
tears fall from them
i sit alone in a dark room
waiting
wondering
as if the outside of the window
is adapting to the way i feel
the city turns dark
gloomy
there is an eerie sound to this
nothingness
no love
nothing to cling to in the middle of the night when you're
scared
just like the moon at night
alone

Evolution
January 1999 (age 14)

I was nothing in their eyes
          shipped over like an animal or a beast
I was nothing to them
          sold off like a piece of property
I was nothing
          getting beat under the whip
          but now

I am something in their eyes
          the entertainer they run home to watch
I am something to them
          their bosses and colleagues
I am something
          their teachers who hold the knowledge
          and soon

I will be everything in their eyes
          their husbands and wives
I will be everything to them
          the president who looks over the country
I will be everything I want to be
          all the dreams my ancestors had
          and all the dreams I have today

Dignity
January 2000 (age 15)

get up girl
you have been beaten down
but you a queen girl
don't let no one steal your crown

lift your head up lady
don't be ashamed
even though your young years
have brought lots of pain

open your eyes young girl
you have much to see
experience what you can
life goes by so quickly

make-up, make-down
June 2000 (age 16)

maybe i'm born with it
maybe it's Maybelline
you say your make-up
makes up
for what's not in my genes
you create flaws so i'll hide what should be seen

you want me
easy
breezy
beautiful
covering-up my beauty inside
by placing a mask on the outside

using Clinique
not showing what's unique
you want me to seek but never find
seek
but never find
search behind
compact doors

you want my foundation
a combination
of confusion and disillusion
gotta imitate your ads
conceal my sadness with your make-up
that just makes me
down

you say, *it's just a little lip gloss girl*
don't exaggerate
well, what if i feel ugly when i awake
already made up my mind to look fake
never feeling i can measure up

as i brush on coats of lies
well, i've cried for too long
and i'm putting down the liner
it won't make me finer
won't make me
feel finer

'cause if that were a fact
at night when i got back
my mascara would be where it was supposed to be
instead of
rolling
down
my cheek

i guess i assigned its position
when i made the transition
of wearing it because i liked it
and needing it to feel
complete

well, it doesn't work- your Revlon
my insecurity still isn't gone
so i'm putting the Mac back
setting myself free

and if i choose to wear make-up
i ain't gon' let it wear me

remote control
June 2000 (age 16)

why you let him
play you like a video
turn you on and off
like a radio
tell you when to go fast and slow
change your channels 'cause he can't stand your show
make you feel so low
have you afraid to say no

why you let him
rewind you
criticize you
hypnotize you
until the screen turns blue
and your life is through

why you let him
tune you
confuse you
and abuse you

reject you
select you
and eject you

why you let him
track you
slap you
and map you

don't know why he do what he do
but you need to
pause you
and rewind you
look at your life before he met you

look back at the moment when you gave him the remote
control
and see how the story unfolds
how instead of asked you were told
what to do and how to feel
and yet you believed that his love was real
and still

fast-forward your life
it appears to be fine
but just like this day and time
you're hurting inside
don't lie

today don't neglect you
reset you
and take back the power
that was held from you

take hold of your life
have it your way
take hold of that remote
and push play

building love
June 2000 (age 16)

i want to love you
but i can't love you like this

from the very moment we kiss
i know it is wrong
but i still try to hold on

i know about you
the things you been through
why you do the things you do

but you know nothing about me
through my eyes you do not see
how i am still trying to find me
and wanting to be the person you want me to be

you don't know how you make me feel
how much i want your dreams to be real
but my feelings i've concealed
and i want to still

but i must let you know
the real me i must show
only then will i truly glow

the poetry of my soul
October 2000 (age 16)

the poetry of my soul
are the words unwritten

the songs of my mind
are the notes unspoken

the dances of my heart
are the steps not taken

the art of my body
is a masterpiece in the making

soul mate
April 2001 (age 17)

strange that i'd like to reach out
and touch my soulmate
sometimes i wish i could determine my fate

can i just sit
and hold you love
can i look into your eyes and know what you're thinking of

i long to long for someone
to long for you
and when we meet don't tell me it's too good to be true

'cause i want the kind of love
that will make the headlines
i want the kind of love no one else can define

when will the day come
when i can give you my heart
when can we gaze into eternity never wishing to part

i never dreamed of
facing forever alone
so please end the suspense and let your face be shown

i love you so much
please don't show up too late
i'll be forever waiting
my sweet soulmate

shadows
February 2002 (age 17)

if all our shadows are the same
why must we be judged by our reflections
why does the world only care about
complexion

the world is a mirror that can't appreciate diversity
and for so long i thought it was a curse to be
mixed
half black and the other half white
but those two colors didn't make me
not quite

last time i checked
black and white made grey
and that's not the color i am today
except over there on that wall
but then grey would be the color of us all

so i'm no different
i'm a product of two shadows
in a world with no reflections where color doesn't show

but in this world color is everyplace
and unlike shadows you can see race
and you can see my imperfections
but still i won't change my reflection
but some go after this correction
as if going in for an inspection

inspected by the mirrors
behind our eyes
the same mirror
in front of a young girl's cries
she thinks she needs to change herself
to somehow qualify

and who was it
that told her that lie
was it her reflection
that whispered to her
that someone she isn't
the world would prefer

'cause she'll be judged by her looks
and not by her actions
but as a shadow
she might have satisfaction
'cause she might have a chance
to be treated equally

and that's really the way
the world should be
but is that just a blind man's fantasy
or can you look at my shadow and say:
you're the same as me

'cause we laugh the same
cry the same
were born the same
and die the same
and since we are here both needed the same
then why can't we be treated the same

criss-cross
February 2002 (age 17)

it's kind of strange how people
meet/ greet
take a seat
and never complete what they might have had

it's kind of strange how paths collide
you're right beside someone you'll never see again

and it looks like i'll never see him again
i can't say he was my friend
just a path i crossed
i kind of wish we crissed
'cause it looks like i missed my chance

looks like i missed the chance to know him
did i react too slow
should i have let him know i want to know him too
intimately
no, not physically
i want our minds to titrate like chemistry

but maybe it wasn't meant to be
maybe he wasn't sent to be
anything but a glance to me
i thought we had a chance to be
something different
but it looks like i'll never see him again

looks like i'll never look into his eyes
i'll always wonder why our first hi
was our first and last goodbye
but i won't cry
paths cross all the time
maybe someday we'll criss
but it looks like i missed my chance

29

love letter to me
June 2002 (age 18)

i demand you to love me
because i am you
i'm your best friend
i've been here
and i know you through and through

look at me. i am beautiful
indulge in my design
between us let me tell you that i am just plain divine
there's no creating a new kind
i am perfectly you
realize this in a hurry
'cause it's time to renew
your essence

i demand you to love me
just look at what i be
a creative, fighter-spirit, learner
being of lovely

don't hide me
disguise me
or bury me beneath fears
but let me beautifully and tenderly
break through and appear

love me
adore me
find me
explore me

take me
arrange me
but don't try to change me
'cause i am you

eternally

and there is no denying me
don't glance beyond the one who loves you most
but notice me
want me
and pull me close

i am your soul
your being
your spirit
yourself
not flawless but perfectly your sense of wealth

so no matter how you live
the most important thing to do
is love me
your best friend
your soulmate
your you

FREEDOM HALL DORMS

———————

△

i move into the dorms at UC Berkeley, about a mile from where i grew up. even so close to home, i feel independent. i still attend my childhood church but sometimes i am resentful of the limitations it imposes on my new life.

♡

i continue to date with a sense of secrecy and find myself falling for one guy in particular: Jasen. even though we don't share the same religious beliefs, he is the first guy who seems to understand me. i hold tight to the possibility that we will be together some day.

Beautiful Stranger
January 2003 (age 18)

I need to tell her
she's beautiful
want her to know that it's true
but she's a stranger
and it's awkward
so i cringe
withhold the truth

And my silence feeds insecurity
expands as my eyes grow green
admiration turns to jealousy
when i refuse to crown her queen

I need to tell her
need her to know
i need to know myself as well
not in my thoughts
but out loud
it becomes real if i tell her she is beautiful

And telling her
tells me the same thing

peach shell
January 2003 (age 18)

a glazed
peach-colored shell
from a Caribbean beach
whispers his unspoken words
he loves me

but
it hurts when i'm with him
'cause
he should have gave God
that shell
instead of me

i've never seen him
praise God for his wonders
so it stings
when he praises
me

daddy's girl
March 2003 (age 18)

you can find her in the club
bottle full of bub
searching for attention 'cause she never had love
she started having sex
and it became a drug
and this is her story so listen up:

Kia twists her hips
as she struts down the street
she's testifyin' she's empty
and wants to find herself complete
  twisting
  strutting
  down the street
searching for looks and compliments
wants them to tell her she's pretty
when she's truly magnificent

but she don't know it

all she knows is she is fine
and not "fine" as in "okay"
but fine as in: "dang baby girl, what's yo name?"
  and she just gives it away

sells her name for some weak 'ol game
sells her name for some
weak 'ol game

reduces her worth to a scrap of paper
degrades herself when all she wants is love—
her father's love

see, when Kia was young
everyone would call her daddy's girl and he could do no wrong

in her eyes
she used to hold his hand
she used to sit in his lap
they used to be best friends
until he left

but
even when he left
Kia was still daddy's girl
but
she had no hand to hold
she had no one to mold her
except the world and her mother
but she was daddy's girl

she was daddy's girl when she was twelve and awkward
but daddy wasn't there to tell her she was still a star in his eyes
knobby knees, braces and all

she was daddy's girl when she was sweet sixteen
but daddy wasn't there to tell her she was growing into a lovely
young woman—beautiful and not just "fine"

and daddy didn't teach her to respect herself
he wasn't there to tell her what them boys were all about
her father could have told her: "Kia, them boys don't really
wanna know how you doing when they ask:
'heeeey, how you doing?'
they waiting for you to say
'fine'
so they can step up to you, recite they weak 'ol line:
'yeah baby, you sho' IS fine.'"

 "NO Kia, you are more than fine, you are mine, my beautiful
baby girl"—but her father never told her that
he left
he left Kia to twist down the street
strutting to feel complete

and one day Tyrone was on his cellular phone
on the corner when Kia switched by
      "hey how you doing?" he asked
      Kia responded, "i'm fine."

and
Tyrone made her feel special
he was five years her senior
and to spell it out for you
he became her father figure
and she even calls him daddy

      "daaaddy, you make me feel like a star"
the star she never was in her father's eyes
      "daaaaddy, can i get the keys to the car?"
but what she really wants are the keys to her father's heart
but he left a long time ago
and Kia wrote him a little note:
      "daddy, i wanted to be your star
      daddy, can you let me know where you are?"

and that is all Kia ever wanted—to find her father's love

wonder how many other daddies' girls
you can find up in the club
bottle full of bub/ searching for attention 'cause they never had
love

Thin Walls
March 2003 (age 18)

We never see you kiss
      and you fight at night

Never a hug or a kiss
      and you fight at night

And in the morning you tell us we are everything and
      everything and
      everything but

      you fight at night

The walls are thin
      The walls are thin
            The walls
            are thin

And they
close in

We discover your flaws too early 'cause
      you fight at night
We could once love so purely but
      you fight at night

And as
years
pass
good times don't seem to last as long

Remember, Dad?
      You used to sing oldies with us
      You used to dance with us
      You used to
            tickle us till we fell

Remember, Mom?
        You used to read with us
        You used to play with us
        You used to make sure
                we were never harmed

Maybe you both thought the walls would shield us
        but
        the walls
        did not protect us like they should

Forget that pain
        we tell ourselves
We are too young
        to battle truth and your lies

Forget that pain

I guess we'll
        cry invisible tears
        behind the walls

Forget that pain

I think we'll just
        believe what we hear at night
                stupid
                        ugly
                stupid
                        ugly

Forget that pain
        forget that pain

But we're grown now
        and we never forgot

The walls did not protect us

caught-up
May 2003 (age 19)

she saunters
the crowded party crowds her
she smiles hesitance
strides innocence
she wants to stay here
and yearns to leave

she yearns to leave

he/touches her sleeve
they dance
and she becomes his one-minute tease
her eyes say/get-your-hands-off-me
but her mouth never moves
she just moves on to another
when the song ends

but the song never ends
the party doesn't stop
and by her eyes i can tell
she's becoming what she's not

the music/gets/faster
she/gets/caught/up/in/the/beat
and/if/this/persists
she/will/get/caught/up/in/the/sheets
scrambles struggles
gets knotted in the sheets
becomes what she's not and
dances to the beat
dances/to/the/beat

knows that
she's worth more than drunken attention
just taking shortcuts /desires pure affection

the crowded party crowds her
she remains uneasy
curly hair whips around her face
and as she turns her head
i notice
she looks
just like
me

HOUSE OF LADIES

toward the beginning of my sophomore year, after much turmoil and internal debate, i decide to leave my church. i believe in God, but don't feel like i can grow in such a restrictive environment. with my newfound autonomy i begin the difficult task of defining for myself what is right and wrong.

without accountability, i am not sure how to run my love life. i feel powerless to assert any real boundaries and am frequently distraught with my decisions regarding men.

utopia hair day
September 2003 (age 19)

today
no good hair/bad hair
just my hair

dark brown
tight curls
frizzy
free

i don't mess with my
tresses
dress up
what's already beautiful

no need to
fry
dye
blow dry
sear
backs of my ears
in attempt to "do" my hair
'cause it's already done

today i don't
primp my hair
and i sho' don't dis' it
i
kiss it

hold her hand
October 2003 (age 19)

i got brown eyes
she got blue
your dark eyes glare
disapprove
as my mother and i
walk by you

so
i stay a few strides behind her
blow away her kisses
reject
her wishes to hold my hand
and instead
i reach for yours
beg you to read my palms
but you
read them wrong

you call me
light-skinned
yellow
tell me my hands aren't
brown enough
to be black
like yours

i long for brownie
not honey skin
wish
mom was black
not white
so you just might
take my hand

but you never intend
to link fingers with me
and while i strain stretch
lunge for your hand
i trip
fall to ground

my mother's palms find me
every crease reminds me
of her intricate love
as she extends her fingers
i vow never to linger as we walk
'cause i'll be right beside her
holding her hand

God
October 2003 (age 19)

if you only live above me
is it possible to love me?

God
for so long i've pictured you
with prescription glasses
squinting
down at the masses
while i pull your leg
and beg
for attention

but when i look toward
the sky
all i feel is neck pain
as i strain to catch
a glimpse of your smile
when all the while
you sit beside me

God
you're my coach
but you run the race with me
if i fall
you kiss me
and tell me to persevere

God
you're my kick-it partner
not afraid to clown if necessary
you
laugh at my jokes
even the ones that ain't funny
and when i
run out of money

47

you buy me nachos at 7-11
ask me
where is heaven?
i laugh 'cause
it's a trick question
heaven is with you
and you
are chillin' right by my side

haiku for music
October 2003 (age 19)

beat blends blue bruises
melodic burgundy tunes
jazz sounds soothe sorrow

more than she can write
December 2003 (age 19)

this poet hurts inside
more
than she
can ever write

her pen can't keep pace with her panic
felt tips run frantic
chase her racing tears
she tries to
wring
her drenching agony
extract it into verse
but only salt grains disperse
scratch the surface of blank sheets

she scratches the surface of
blank sheets
wonders

why did he leave her
blank
leave her empty

wordless.

he don't even know
she's a
poet

she wants to soak pages
with her grief
but
her tears are not ink
will not express her story rhythmically

how can she
retell
the sound of her sobs
as they echo off bathroom walls

this poet
hurts inside
more
than she can ever write
despite
how she strains
she cannot squeeze her pain
through the tip of her
pen

phone call to dad after seven months
February 2004 (age 19)

Brenda
from desktop
support
answers my call
instead of you

wrong number

so much for dialing
by heart

water balloon bombs
March 2004 (age 19)

out of the blue
a
green
water balloon
plummets
from
high-rise
dorms

smacks
on the
asphalt
before us

halts our poetry session

i squint upward
wonder
what faceless coward felt brave enough
to harass a group of
peaceful people

makes me wonder too
how easily
bombs slip from fingers
aimed at blurry faces
a few feet down
wonder how many
poetry sessions they disrupt

if those same people
elevator down
six floors
stare into our eyes
join our crosslegged circle

hear our words

would they still burst balloons in our faces

or would the water dribble out
leak
make silent puddles
on the ground
by their feet
till all that's left
is soggy plastic

solo
April 2004 (age 20)

forget a duet
i groove onstage
solo
in front of an audience of three
receive a standing ovation from
i
myself
and me

see me
April 2004 (age 20)

you say you want to
see me
and i think
finally
someone wants to
understand me
wants to
study my scars
gaze at my grin
wants to be my friend

you say you want to
see me
and i think
well let's meet
how 'bout at sunrise
lemon sky
abundant light—
the better to
see me with
right?

you say you want to
see me
but your words
don't come out easy
'cause the last thing you want
is light

i never ask
why
why if you want to
see me
so much
do you only call at night?

LA CASA EN LA COLINA

SAN JOSE, COSTA RICA | AGE 20-21

in the second semester of my junior year, i leave the United States for the first time in my life to study abroad. i live with a host family for six months and take classes at the University of Costa Rica. i am still figuring out where my values and beliefs lie and hope the distance will help me change my unhealthy habits.

i plan to take a break from dating while in Costa Rica, but a couple of guys catch my interest. my heart is still connected to Jasen and even though we haven't talked consistently over the months, i am convinced things can work out between us.

flimsy
March 2005 (age 20)

never thought
i would learn to treat my body
like loose-leaf paper
pass it around like sign-in sheet

never thought the word no would get choked
in my throat
afraid to speak my mind
'cause he might not like me
anymore

never thought that having sex would be so
easy
simple
expected
a given

i know from the minute we step inside
the minute he slides his hand
just a little lower than the waistline
i know from the second
he pays
attention to me
the second he pays
admission for me

but i deny it in my head
play pretend
trick my mind into thinking we can just
be friends
talk and cuddle all night
watch a movie all the way through

trick my mind into thinking that if something does happen

i won't feel guilty in the morning
or changed

ev-er-y-single-time i act like
this night
won't go the same way
his gradual advances
my powerless noooo's
and an ending i know all too well

i want to go back
back to when befriending guys was easier
a movie was a movie
a conversation was a conversation
a slumber party involved slumber

i never realized
sex would change things so much
that it would be so
hard to stop once i started
even if it ain't right for me
even if it doesn't feel healthy

never thought
i'd be at war with myself
a full-on battle between
                    the pressure of his advances
          my desire to be close to someone but not-that-close
                    my inability to say no
          my fear of ruining the mood
                    my own lust and curiosity

i never thought i'd feel this flimsy

like loose-leaf paper in the wind
blown across pavement
tangled in tree branches

59

stuck in gutter grate

forever floating
when will i take a stance
when will i do what's best for me
when
will i outgrow these paper wings

single flower
March 2005 (age 20)

bring me a
single flower
one lifelong love
better than
a bouquet
any day

walk of shame
May 2005 (age 21)

she limps into house
with 6AM walk
tryna
play it off but

she can't just act
all innocent

them
early morning
high heels
is tellin' all her
secrets

tan
May 2005 (age 21)

she got herself a tropical tan
a topical tan
a beachside loungin' sunblockable tan

she got a take-home tan
a returnable tan
a look-how-dark-i-am-in-this-photo tan

a seasonal tan
a reasonable tan
a well-earned-vacational, feasible tan

a mild tan
an in-style tan
a fade-away-after-a-while tan

peach shell part II
June 2005 (age 21)

you hand me a
glazed
peach-colored shell
from a Caribbean beach
you love me

i travel to distant blue waters
run my hands through rough sands
scan the shore
the ocean floor
explore
and find nothing

so i send sea mist
to kiss your lips
grains of black sand
to slip through your hands
and fall
where you stand

i shout to the wind
whisper to waves
i sail these secrets to your shore
to assure you
i love you too

when i say no
July 2005 (age 21)

i say
no

you don't
obey

and afterward i
beg
you to
stay

ask you
to
hug my pain
away

when
you
the one
that caused it

TELEGRAPH APARTMENT

———————

i return from overseas with great anticipation for my senior year. i move in with one of my best friends who had studied abroad with me in Costa Rica. still exploring God's role in my life, i join a religious group on campus and begin attending a new church. this time around, my spiritual experience feels authentic. i am part of a positive community that challenges me but gives me room to figure things out on my own.

i start to question my infatuation with Jasen since he doesn't reciprocate my feelings.

marry him girl
January 2006 (age 21)

you only met him once
known him for three weeks
but you phone him daily
and i listen to you speak

and
he gives you full body laughter
intrigues you fo(u)r
hours

and
your eyes ain't ceased to shimmer since the day you met
your eyes
they glow like snowflakes under winter sunsets

and when it's wet outside
you call him
and if you trip and fall
you call him

for three
weeks
straight
he
fulfills your desires
through telephone wires
imagine
sparks and fire
when you see him again

marry him girl
say yes
it only makes sense
you exhaust me with your
what-does-this-mean

your
what-should-i-infer
i roll my eyes
he's yours
you don't have to do anything
don't have to
press out your curls or
dumb down your vocabulary
don't have to
tune down your spirituality
with him
you are exactly you
just say "I do"

i don't understand what you're waiting for
marry him girl.

car trouble blues
February 2006 (age 21)

he say that he love me, even lend me his car
i said, he show me that he love me, give me keys to his car
but i drive away solo, i want the keys to his heart

i feel special in his front seat when we drivin' through town
make me feel special ridin' shotgun when we roll through town
but next day he carpoolin', drivin' other girls around

he needa tell me what he want 'cause he steady switchin' gears
he need to tell me what he want 'cause he confuse me shiftin' gears
and if that boy keep stallin', gotta find me some new wheels

home sweet home
February 2006 (age 21)

I.

six months
i world travel
hang clothes in foreign closet
dream between unfamiliar sheets

homesick

but not for
two-ten south thirteenth street
or three-thousand-nine mcgee
but for one-four-three love street

homesick for you

II.

you the only one
i write love poems to
you my backyard
front porch too

you make me feel like
childhood
popsicles and hopscotch

you make me feel free
like riding banana seat bike down jefferson street

you make me feel
woman
bubble baths and candles

you make me beautiful
like butterscotch sweet and strong
like evening gown and shawl
wrapped in your arms

you make me feel like
me
afro puff and ripped jeans
like handmade dangly earrings
like watching sunday night tv
in dancing clothes

with you i'm
child
and still feel
grown
with you i'm
home

III.

our first embrace
a housewarming

your smile
a summertime barbeque

your heart
a mailbox
stuffed with my love poems

your shoulder
a placemat that say
home sweet home

git it together
March 2006 (age 21)

giiiirl
if you 'ont git yoself up
outta that
dirty nasty
funk you in
i'm liable to
tell yo' pastor
den
imma tell somebody mama

girl
you needa git it together
stop
sportin' them
droopy pink sweatpants 'round the house
stop avoidin' people like they the plague 'n stuff
stop catchin' attitudes 'n being rude 'n
all that mess
'cause you gon' turn around 'n be friendless

girl
when you
funk-less
you illuminate rooms
perfume space with your laughter
you got God's aroma
seepin' through your pores

so girl
you jus' needa shake it off one good time
holla at a scripture girl
take it to God girl
but jus' come on outta that funk girl

dang!

hair politics
March 2006 (age 21)

today i got my hair twisted
so you stop
say
      hey sista

but when i wear my hair straight
you walk straight past me
guess i ain't
      family
no more

creation story
March 2006 (age 21)

in the beginning
God said
let there be Alicia
and
San Francisco city officials
bulldozed and paved
a street
so my parents would meet
and then there was me

late night poem series
March-July 2006 (age 21/22)

I.

march 5, 2006 11:49pm

i do not want
sweet nectarines
nor do i desire your
kisses
i just want to
hug myself to sleep
watch raindrops smear window
breathe in
absorb dark sky
through my skin

II.

april 6, 2006 2:11am

i miss you.
i really do
and maybe i just get
late night lonely
but i just wanted to tell you
i love you.
with my dull heartaches
and blue room blues
wish i could love you as much as i say i do
like love you in the daylight
or love you on the moon
i want to be your morning bad-breath kiss
your whisper-to at events
want to be a smile on your caller ID

wondering if you busy
worrying you won't answer the phone
be the worst feeling in the world

III.

april 6, 2006 2:13am

maybe you just an idea or
a lost cause
maybe i shouldn't
treasure hunt you anymore
maybe you'll never be my Valentine
or Anniversary
maybe you just the sweetest love poem
written for someone
other than me.
life. never how we plan it
how we wish it. dream it.
that's why i often wish i never
daydreamed you into my perfect man.
better to erase you from my thoughts
for the chance that you could be my
sweet surprise
my never-thought-it-would-happen man

IV.

april 7, 2006 2:34am

note to my roommate:
how can silence
sting more than a slap
don't you know that every
nonchalant greeting

every cancelled girl talk
is a punch in the heart
right in the spot where
our friendship used to be

it's not that you're mean to me
only that you won't giggle
with me anymore
won't volunteer information
all you ever did was run tongue marathons
now you don't even jog
what did i do to make
you so out of shape

V.

april 7, 2006 2:38am

i'm in a late night poetry groove
got starlight make my pen move
something about dark rooms
and dark corners
and dark circles
that make me want to scribble
dark spots on paper

VI.

april 7, 2006 2:59am

i don't miss your poetry/ don't miss your sweet laughter/don't
miss your late night phone calls or your online
emails/i don't miss your seashells/ i don't miss your forehead
or forearm kisses/ don't miss your late night La
Burrita trips/ i don't miss your birthday parties/ don't miss your
friends/ i don't miss hearing you sing off tune
i just miss you

VII.

july 19, 2006 12:46am

i wished you there tonight
at the poetry spot
and the moment i saw you i thought
        there goes my soulmate
and when you got behind the mic
it felt like
me and you
together forever and
you stared into my eyes as you recited
memorized verse
        i felt you
and i felt every year in that moment
every late night food run
every cancelled date
every front seat handhold as we drove
you took me down reminiscence lane
        it's funny how close
        and so far i feel from you
you
        have skinny fingers and big knuckles
        and you snore at night. breathe
        heavy when you sleep. you love
        past your capacity and you
        mr. cool nerd and you goofy
        and i love you
                enough that i can't stop saying it
                and i can't stop feeling it

i know i write too many poems about you
that i love you too hard sometimes when
i may not even know what love is

i just know that i felt full
tonight standing in your presence

all i wanted was an i-ain't-seen-you-in-forever-hug
an i-don't-care-who's-watching-it's-just-me-and-you hug

i am not satisfied looking like one
of your adoring fans
a hi-bye, loved-your-poetry girl
i ain't satisfied
hearing you publicize your relationships
over mic. 'cause it ain't about me

i just know:
i didn't arrive with you
didn't leave with you
but i came home smelling like you

i know
just because we soulmates
don't mean we will be together
you got you and you
don't think like me
maybe don't feel the way i do and i
know
you got your rappin' thing
your traveling thing
your selling cds performing thing
your no time for Alicia thing

it's okay. it really is.
we soulmates
but in this time and space you done
spaced out and used your time in
another place
> i will never force you to love me
> i won't live life waiting for you

but i'll still float to ceilings when you enter the room
i'll still float to ceilings when you enter the room

cannery
April 2006 (age 22)

you cannot
can me
like summer peaches
shelve me
out of reach
and
expect me to
wait for some
snowy day of yours

you cannot
vacuum seal my mouth
expect me to shout
airtight love songs
at the pop of my seal

i do not
sweeten with age
i do not flourish in
dark corners

i won't let you
store me
away
seclude me
you can not
preserve me
nor
make me your
jellied treat

i am
plump summer peach
fresh for the picking
ripe for the eating

and i'll be damned
if i sit around
wait
till my expiration date

i'd rather find myself
rotten
than to be forgotten
in your basement
cannery

rush rebellion
April 2006 (age 22)

tomorrow i want to
beachtown stroll and
stop at red lights
smile at strangers
smell the flavor of Jamba juice on their tongues
look friends in the eye
instead of whiz fly
past them
i want to rebel against sidewalk
fastlane traffic

but instead
i wake up flustered
snatch bagel out of toaster
suck down Capri Sun
dash run around house
throw on dirty laundry pants
and arrive
panting
to class

telegraph obstacle course
May 2006 (age 22)

no.
i don't want your meaningless scrap of paper
don't want your
blondie's pizza discount coupon
don't hand me invitations to parties
no, i'm not looking for an internship
i don't want to sign up for the revolution
don't need a new credit card
or hot tracks on a burned cd
and *pleeease* don't try to holla at me

i just want to get home

alameda county fair
May 3, 2006 (age 22)

the fair. my favorite memory. every summer without fail we hop on afternoon train and spend true family summertime. my mom my sisters and i. we stay there till night time falls, till the last bus calls.

'cause at the fair, sticky caramel corn scents the air. we gaze at glazed candied apples and pastel cotton candy. eat thick-battered corn dogs and chow down at the all-you-can-eat diner. sip strawberry sweet water. chew on the left over chunks stuck at the bottom of mom's cup of agua fresca.

at the fair mom doesn't stress about the rent. all that matters are hourly talent shows under the big tent featuring hyper hypnotists and blonde girls in aqua blue leotards. dancing like they're on Star Search.

in the commercial tent, we don't care we can't afford the appliances. we stroll wide-eyed, wander booth to booth. gawk at balding man, watch him smear oil on carpet and dissolve it away with magic spray. we never buy the products, just watch them try to sell us non-stick pans when we just want free stir-fry samples.

we wait in line for hours for free-with-admission concerts. no-name country singers, Lou Rawls and of course—fall in love with The Temptations, The Spinners, City High, and even Carrot Top.

at the fair nothing matters but what is right in front of us. icees and instant photos. barnyard animals and print-out astrology notes. salt water taffy and fireworks.

my favorite memory. the fair. where we spend true family summertime, my mom my sisters and i. we stay there till night time falls. till the last bus calls.

but we'd stay there a lifetime if we could.

85

smile bright
May 2006 (age 22)

you smile
and lemons
pucker
sun squints
bashful bananas
shed their skin
and blonde tulips
arch their backs and
worship

you smile
and corn start poppin'
burst into golden
confetti
celebrate your
divine grin

your smile like that
traffic light
between green and
red
got people
accelerating
to catch you

you smile
and
lemonheads chatter
clack between teeth
gossip 'bout your gleam
'cause your smile
so lemon
so sweet
should be baked in
meringue pie

your smile
so luminous
so bright
it got everything
that's yellow
begging
shoutin'
hollerin'
for mercy

ice cream
June 2006 (age 22)

our first date
you want ice cream
something sweet
a little summertime treat

i imagine us
cones in hand
on rainbow-sherbet Telegraph Ave
all smiles and swirls
not a care in the world

just dulce boy
with sweet sweet girl

we shoulda just ate ice cream

shoulda walked to Yogurt Park
drove to Ben & Jerry's
paid three-fifty for something sweet
a little summertime treat

instead
we chill at my pad
i lick the groove of your neck
you cup your hand
around my breast
and we both leave empty

no maple cone sweetness
just the bitterness of
tasting desert
before we even had dinner

talking to you
July 2006 (age 22)

talking to you be like
candy treat
like red licorice
            sweet
like the insides of
sour patch kids
and tangy
you make my taste buds
celebrate
from the
flavor of
your voice

when i talk to you
i'm hyper kid
burst into giggles
you make me
wiggle and
superball bounce off walls

you got me on a
sugar high that don't crash

talking to you is like
twisting top off sprite
you got me
lemon-shocked
and limed
even at 4am (my time) and
6am (your time)

i said
you got me
lemon-shocked
and limed

'cause each time we speak
your spirit refresh me like citrus
you never miss a chance to
mist me with the truth
no matter how
sour or bitter
it tastes on my tongue
with you i can reveal the
true me
like grapefruit without peelings
like bare tangerine and
you stimulate my mind
even though we
two time zones away
you turn my zzz's into zeal
with your zest
i forget about rest
and sleep
and that i gotta be up
at six
in the morning

'cause talking to you makes
wall clocks run ahead of schedule
and earth spin faster on her axle
time must've
joined the track team
been practicing 100 meter repeats
'cause three hours
ain't never raced by this fast before

and conversation never tasted this good before
each night i talk to you
feels like
Sunday dinner
smothered chicken
mac & cheese
red beans and rice

90

and every conversation is seasoned
just right
you give me sound
solid advice
you comfort food for my soul
and i always want
a to-go plate to bring home

talking to you
got me on orbitz.com
searching for the cheapest flight
that will get me there
tonight

ice water conversation
July 2006 (age 22)

you got me
refreshed
like free
ice water at the bar
you mr. calm and collected
calmly collected my number and
i hope you call real soon

your smile
refresh me because you seem genuine
and ain't nothing like
ice water conversation
the kind that make you go aaahhh

and why did you kiss me on the cheek
when i left
was it just a formality or
do you think i'm cute
it was so nice to meet you
and i can't wait till you call
so i can take a sip of that
cool cool conversation

fly
July 2006 (age 22)

i call you before i board planes
so don't that make it plain
to see i love you
you my last goodbye before i fly
last hug before i soar

but
maybe i should just depart
maybe i should just say my
airplane gate goodbye to you

maybe i shouldn't cry before
flights or
tote you like carry-on bag
'cause you getting too bulky
too big
maybe i can check you in
or maybe you'll be lost luggage
somewhere in Alabama
me in California
maybe you lost forever 'cause i
never labeled or tagged you as mine
you got sent on different plane
different destination

but i'll be fine with no
baggage to claim
because
ain't like you ever carry me on with you
ain't like you ever carry on talking about
me
ain't like you'll miss me
or run after to catch me

so maybe i'll pack light next flight

maybe my itinerary just say me

and maybe next trip i'll wave a soaked-tissue goodbye
yeah maybe without you i'll cry

but maybe
just maybe
without you
i'll fly

sister silence
August 2006 (age 22)

i want to tell you
that your beauty
makes rainforests
hum sweet songs
and waterfalls laugh
when they trickle and
fall down mountain

i want to say
that i admire how God designed you
wish i could uproot every insult
planted into your heart
take back every tangled dirty lie
anyone ever told you
and sow seeds of strength
truth resilience

i never told you that
i love having a younger sister
loved helping you with art projects and math homework
i wish you would ask me advice about life
about how to love and forgive

i want to tell you
don't resent anyone
so much
that you become them
you have your whole life ahead of you and
forgiveness taste so sweet on your tongue

i want to tell you
sorry
for
standing by and
watching you cry

when dani
all muscle brute of a girl
wrestles you to ground
presses your face into the cold snow
and i sit there
numb   afraid
or when
leslie threatens to hit you
and i still sit
next to her in the van
instead of you

i want you to know
if i could take it back
i would
and if i could be attacked
instead of you
i would
'cause i never want to see you in pain
forgive me
i was
young girl
confused
trying to find myself
didn't know the meaning of blood
that it's thicker than
winter frozen water
didn't know that while i ran toward
snow i forgot about the mountain
you
my sister
strong and mighty
you
an Everest to climb sometimes
but worth the struggle

i want you know
you're lovable

i remember
when you were a baby
i must have been three
i used to sit and watch you
and kiss your tiny feet
i loved you so much
my dear little sister
don't know when or why
i ever stopped telling you

ALICIA ZAKON

CARIBBEAN CRASH PAD

---

after my graduation ceremonies, i enroll a final semester to study abroad again. this time, i know what i want out of my stay in a new country and it turns out to be one of the best experiences of my life. i feel free and genuine and am more inspired than i have been in a long time.

before arriving in Barbados, i pray to find a special friend that i can connect with on a deep level. i end up meeting him—Zeke—and accidently fall in love.

cucaracha
October 2006 (age 22)

roaches don't
fly
in California
they shuffle across floors
and they come in nice
petite sizes
a gentle rolled-newspaper smack
will send them to their graves

but here in Barbados
macho cockroaches
bench press 250 pounds
and dare you to cross their paths
in dark alleyways of your kitchen

one raided my room last night
didn't respond to my screams
just stood in my doorway like
girl please

we have a staredown
like old western movie
roach approaches
i snatch my covers and pillow
dart for the door
sleep in dorm lobby

i know i'm scary
but let's see what you do
when a gansta Bajan roach
comes and steps to you

cover-up
October 2006 (age 22)

when UVA rays
sting our pupils
we buy designer glasses
to safety goggle our eyes

don't question why
just ask
do they come in purple and white

cover-up
instead of finding
the root
as long as we looking cute

I's
October 2006 (age 22)

like a good father
you want to teach your daughters to drive
want to show us the rules of the road
want us to see what life's like in the driver's seat

you done traveled worldwide. many journeys. too many wrong
turns. you want to show us where we should never venture.

you know bitter backroads all too well. shady shortcuts. roads of regret.

you want to show us the freeways

but we scared
just like you, 'cause you not always sure which way to go.
sometimes you end up where you don't want to be.

but you still teach us to drive
so we won't live in passenger seat

forgotten
October 2006 (age 22)

maybe if i turn my phone to silent
i won't wait for your call so
desperate-like

maybe i can forget you
like tasteless paper

i feel crumpled

and now you see me wrinkled never
fresh again in your eyes

an unedited poem
a throwaway

you have no words for me now it seems
what happened to daily text messages
and phone calls at night
maybe you forgot about the sparkle
in my eye   maybe i'm just some fallen
star to you
wished on then forgotten
plenty more in the galaxy

i wanted us to be a special constellation
not just a jumble of confusion

matador
November 2006 (age 22)

she
soggy-faced
draped in red
swimming in crimson fabric
clings to her matador's shoulder
finds comfort in the certainty of death

she knows her time is short
but she
smothered in ruddy lies
got distracted by
the swift flick of his cape
the slight curving of his arm
'round her waist

she collapses onto to ruby sheets
slippery silky heat
forgets that he
matador
is a cold killer
not her lover
that he handles swords
not bouquets of red roses
that he is incapable of loving her
(even if he loved her)
that his only promise
is certain death

she
clothed in crimson
knows this
she just wants
something besides dyed fabric
to cling to

#laundryandlovenotes

so when the moment comes
for him to plunge dagger into heart
she doesn't run
she just bleeds her scarlet blood
the color of red red roses

ZR protest
November 2006 (age 22)

a dollar fifty
will get you
to town
'cause everyone
needs to shop

a dollar fifty will
get you home
safely
get you home
maybe
or not

this is for anyone
harassed on a ZR bus
groped in a ZR seat
made to feel
cheap like silver coins
that clink in pocket
but we are more than just
heads and tails for someone to
flip when they want to

we will not
exchange
harassment
for transit

they say
one-fifty
but we say
two feet be
just fine
prefer walking
over compromise

we shout NO in protest
we screech-halt ZR tires
because one silver dollar and
and two quarters
is more than we can afford
when we have to
cower in corners

we will not exchange
harassment
for transit

will not barter our values
negotiate
beg
we
hold tight our silver change
hear it clang in our pockets
as we march in protest
until something
changes

island love
December 2006 (age 22)

barbados sweet barbados
i remember dreaming of you
wondering if i would like you
would i
uncover secrets tucked in my heart
while safe in your arms

i imagined what you would think when
you met me
        artsy California girl
        bulging luggage
        insecure
you
        endless sandy shore
        so sure of yourself
almost feels like you know me
when we greet
give me sunkiss on my
cheek

over the months i get to know you
        your sticky morning breath
        your noonday laughs
        your midnight moonlight
you teach me
to take my mind off ticks and tocks
'cause "let's meet at noon"
can mean six o' clock
you teach me patience
how to live in the moment

and i breathe in each second
dance the day away with you
read and write you poetry
show you my dramatic side

talk with you all night

you special
deep
takes a while to get to know you
but as time passes you let me explore
your endless country fields
your secrets in closed-off caves

sunsets with you feel more magnificent
stars a little closer at night
i can almost touch them taste them

and i don't care when your mood shifts and
grey storm clouds cross your skies
life can't always bring sunshine

i'm not supposed to like you so much
when thinking of return flights and
how many nights i have left
until i leave you

supposed to stay distant
so i don't get hurt
or attached
so i can avoid the discomfort of missing you
not supposed to weave
memories and
songs together
so that future plays
will remind me of the way
you smell

i know i must say farewell
but it don't feel right
it should be me
forever
with island paradise

mahogany memories
December 2006 (age 22)

i remember
     long gaze-at-galaxy nights
     first kiss on campus rooftop

i remember
     friday night photoshoots
     and you

     stir-fry ginger chicken
     extra old rum and coke
     from Esso
     neosoul
     tears that escape your eyelids unknowingly
     as you yawn
     the way your eyes light when you tell
     a story from home
     your innocent boy laugh

sweet sepia memories
the kind that make your heart beat stronger when thinking of them
you were my restful retreat
a shoulder to lean on
someone to share art with
laugh with
watch boondocks
talk about God and spiritual gifts

i always wonder
if i dramatized it all
if those feelings were real
if those moments were as magical as i made them
maybe i saw you for someone you weren't
i see you dark brown and you just clear
see you deep
and you just near the surface

110

i hope you cling to something in life
like i grasp at these memories
hope you find your special someone
and never let the taste of them
leave your skin

MOM'S COUCH

---

upon arrival from Barbados, i move in with my mom and begin the rough transition into the "real world." i exhaust myself with various part time jobs, become actively involved at my church, and find time to travel. i yearn for stability and a clearer sense of direction.

a few months after my return, i start conversing online with a guy i had met during my last couple weeks in Barbados. we develop a strong connection and have much in common, including our religious beliefs. after five months of talking and visiting, we commit to dating long distance. although i care about my boyfriend a lot, i often doubt if i should be in a relationship. to further complicate things, i am not completely over Zeke.

he wasn't you
December 2006 (age 22)

for Lee

i'm waiting for bus 88
half past eight in the
morning
Sacramento and University
wishing for a ride

and i swear he looks like you from the side

same black car
young black guy with fitted hat
leaned back stance

i tighten my glance like it's not almost
nine in December and
like
i can't remember that
last month i bought black
pants at Ross to wear to your funeral

i squint into car like
maybe i'll see a baseball
mitt in
backseat
know that you're headed to a game
and i'll call you
later ask you
why i've never seen you play
after five
years of friendship

he looks like you from the side but he's
not you
and i want to scream

114

scream so
the light won't turn green
he won't turn left
this will all be a dream and when i wake up your
right-side look alike will be gone and you'll see me at the bus
stop
pull over
offer me a ride

like old times

to the man that loves me
January 2007 (age 22)

i wish i could play card tricks with my emotions. turn my diamond like for you into red heart love. wish i could see you like i did that first night at the club. you, a sharp black spade. me, so gleeful that you paid me attention.

wish there was a way to change my mentality
'cause it seems like you're too much
man to be letting slip by
so easily

strings attached
January 2007 (age 22)

we had a tangled interaction
some sort of twisted attraction
and like a hemline i was taken in

you stitched a quiltwork straight to my heart
knowing
i had to depart
soon
        and these strings you stitched
        still attach
        me to you

i tried my best to
just do the homeylover thing
be free and loose
safe from the noose of love
and concern
but somehow i got snagged in
your yarn

and now there is
        nothing but string
intricate weave. floss
        between teeth. thing you pull from sweater that's
        holding everything together

        without you i unravel

i want to tightrope back to your breezy apartment
where we walk barefoot and stare up at white wooden ceiling
dreaming

i want to buckle up a harness and zipline back
to your island
cross caribbean seas

what
can i do
with these strings

i thought i could unlace you over time but this
double knot between us just won't untie

i know.
i shouldn't be attached to
your fingertips
i am not your string puppet but
i can't help but think what luck i always get
        to be bound to those
        who don't love   me
        to be foolish enough not to
        consider the miles this string extends

        the frailty

i wonder
why. why am i tied to you and who made this knot so
tight. can you loosen it. like too-tight shoelaces. i
know we're in two different places but
        let's just
        strum these strings like guitar
        like violin
        let's tighten these strings
        and make sweet music
        again

Haiti: strangerfriend
April 2007 (age 23)

Haiti.
i barely know you.
you like a church member sitting a few pews down.

i see you watching the preacherman. your countenance stoic almost.

i want to talk to you but everyone's humming and you're
looking the other way.

i don't understand you yet i'm so close i can smell the color of
your blouse. i know what you look like after a
shower.

but i can't hear you. can't speak your tongue.

i want to snatch your thoughts like a greedy preacherman.
usurp an offering only you know how to give.

but what can i give you. how many ways can i lay in your
arms. are my cheeks ample enough to let your tears
roll down them, backside of palms strong enough to smudge
them away.
there's no time for pain. no time to wallow in sorrow like
tepid bathwater. we got rivers to cross and
heavy loads of coal to prop on our shoulders. we have roads to
tread and no one in our way. a life must be lived while we have
breath

no time for tears or water breaks.

you step in rhythm to the beat of kompa. wade through the
heat that tries to tell you life is over.

you take your place in line and wait. you move and keep
moving. howl if you need to. cry if you get the chance at the break

of day but you never let the day break you into two halves you can never piece together. you stay whole even when the seams of you start to weaken.

Haiti.
i barely know you. but you are no longer a stranger. just a long lost friend i will never forget.

midair thoughts:
April 2007 (age 23)

1.

traveling back across time zones. running laps across the sky.
fighting against the night.

2.

la republica dominicana. i think this was the first time i felt like crying
when having to leave a country. premature, only a 10-day trip. felt like i was
velcrostripped out of the tropics. almost found myself at home among sepia
skin tones and español. una guagua bus ride y platanos.

3.

i liked when people said i look like my sister. enjoyed that most folks couldn't
tell who was older, who was younger. our roles switched from time to time & i
realized two year gap starts to close as you get older.

4.

strange how we try to have this lil' western world way up here, even in
turbulent skies. TV screen showing David Letterman, Hollywood cinema,
sit-coms. and we sit. calm. like it's normal to
grow wings and fly on a Wednesday.

why do miracles become dull when rerun.

5.

how come we don't create another world in the sky? escape from
groundbound prejudice.

remember what the sound of your breath feels like before you shove in ear
buds. lift the arm rest divider and sleep on the shoulder of a stranger. give up
your first class seat to an elderly woman.

and why conduct business while floating? close your laptop and
watch the aerial view of the sunset.

6.

i stay so connected that i've memorized electronic devices better than the
pattern of the veins on the back of my hands. i can fumble in the night and type
an email but i couldn't tell you what kinds of
love notes my left hand could write you in the dark.

7.
nine-ish in the sky. clouds look like crushed ice. city lights glow
like snowcone syrup fallen to the bottom of the cup.

8.

slight curve of the earth lets you see how woman the globe is.

countdown
May 2007 (age 23)

for Heidi

in
Costa Rica
you used to count down the days till
we left that dreadful place
January 21st
170 days left
you roll colones and your eyes
sigh as we trudge uphill to the university
next day you ink 169 on your hand
and we all think you should
live in the moment   enjoy yourself
lose count
and after a while
you do

but now
i wonder
where did those numbers go
how come nobody
knew
how few days we had left on earth
with you

i never knew
that reggae sweat night at club in LA
was where we'd have our last conversation
would be the last time i saw you grace the dance floor

i would have stuck by your side the whole night

i would have pencil recorded every joke you told and
cleaned your fingernails
anything but take you for granted

you leave me with unanswered questions
like where is the
pink nail polish you bought me for my 21st birthday
and
will our hug last me a lifetime

missing my boo
August 2007 (age 23)

i miss being in your gaze
all we have now are web pages
msn windows

i want to slide a note through
the slot in your living room window

want your smile in my California
you are so cute
your ways
i love you
or at least i think i do
from thousands of miles away

why would God make our
daylights begin at different hours

i want another rain shower we can sit under
in the car

another front seat conversation
another confession
another pinch

one more kiss on my
elbow

something to show my kids

a text message

LITTLE COTTAGE IN THE HOOD

———————

BERKELEY, CA | AGE 24-25

i move out of my mom's house, begin teaching at my old high school, and attend night classes for my teaching credential. i am overwhelmed but inspired, and still trying to answer the ever-looming question of my life's purpose.

after a year, my boyfriend and i break up because we start to feel like our lives are traveling down two distinct paths.

why i'm glad you stood me up today
August 2008 (age 24)

you prove yourself this time
you prove what i should already know
          you're selfish beyond measure

i waited two years to see your face
wondered if a simple embrace could make up for
two years of disengagement
wondered if it would transport me back to those memories
i cherish but try desperately to forget

i've allowed you to invade my thoughts
plague my life with what-ifs
and daydreams of how you and i
should have/could have/might have
worked out

even though when i left your country
you didn't even pretend to care about how my life unfolds
don't email for updates
don't pay me no matter

you are selfish beyond measure

you tell me just two days ago
how you recall each moment we spent together
how you miss our late night talks
how you still remember my cell number by heart
and the time you lifted me over your head on the dance floor

you say
we should do lunch before you leave
i say
i'm free
and you call me today
at lunchtime

tell me
i'll be there in an hour
and three hours later
no call

not as if i sat there waiting for you
i actually prayed you wouldn't show up
that you wouldn't find enough consideration to even call
'cause now
only now
can i truly rest on the fact that you were never for me
now
i can set you aside when i think about my future
now
i can reframe the past
knowing that what we had was never
meant to be longlasting
how could i ever be with someone so disengaged and inconsiderate

you're not even kind enough to be rude
shove me aside
make me rust in hate for you
would make life a little easier

instead
you choose sweet talk and reminiscing
pull me aside at the party for conversation
and you pull my heartstrings even if you didn't mean to

why did you even suggest lunch today
if you didn't want to
i don't need your food

truly i'm getting over you
i'm pissed
but glad
ever so glad that you proved yourself
a selfish one

129

thank you for standing me up
because now
i have the strength
to leave you
and the idea of you
behind
for good

on the brink of change
November 4, 2008 (age 24)

"We are the ones we have been waiting for." - June Jordan

walking home from voting
pride creeps up inside me. i see young
black boy holding the door for
his mother—it's just a regular moment
but all of a sudden it's like
i can see just a glimpse
more of humanity
sense of camaraderie
like we're in on a great secret

this is a moment to be celebrated
and i want to be elated already

a young black woman, natural
short 'fro walks out of Sweet
Adeline bakery. i pass her
doning my "i voted" sticker
she says two words and
i am transported
      "peace, sista"
and suddenly i feel
like a part of history. some
nostalgic memory
some magic
moment. some change. a little
validation. a little
openness. a little of what
we all seek.
      peace.
and
to be a part of a loving
family.
      "peace, sista"

i smile back at her
both of us knowing the
monumentalness of the
moment. pure and
untainted. black pride and
possibilities.

we are the ones
we have been waiting for.

cinema
December 2008 (age 24)

you stand
6'3"
chocolate skinned
edible grin
such swagger
tall
dark
handsome

noticed by many
so how
honored i must be
when you notice
me

do you know
sometimes
i scratch plaque off my teeth
i pluck stray hairs from my chin
eat oatmeal and applesauce
i curl up to cliché romantic comedies and
sometimes i get scared when alone in public restrooms
so much that i flee toward the exit
heart racing

how can you think i'm fly

with you i become illuminated silver-screen version of myself
a clumsy cinderella
suddenly i'm leading lady like
kate hudson or kirsten dunst
i'm smart and sexy all the time
poetic and deep
swept off my feet

and i think i see glitter floating by
the whole thing is a script
our first unsuspected midnight kiss on rooftop
your "secret spot you come to think"

scripted

your silly text messages
telling me i'm cute
but you've never seen me
pluck hair from my face
how are you even
qualified to make such a statement
you don't even know me

yet somehow i think you're my prince
like you're going to marry a
study abroad student and
carry me to a castle far away

the more i get in character the more i forget
my plane ticket home
and how unsexy i feel when
you stand me up
or appear uninterested

i keep replaying scenes in my head
wishing for an alternate ending
praying for someone
to lift me out of my unhappiness
but there is no
tall-handsome
there is just me
talented yet
regular californian

i fail to see
you were always just regular too

change your clothes four times before going out
distance yourself from family
you stink after a workout
human like me

and you will never be my savior
this is not "maid in manhattan"
i am alicia not j-lo
you're just a guy trying to have fun

and you are just a scene in my life
you were never the plot

txt msg

January 2009 (age 24)

tired of txting. tired of misinterpreted msgs. tired of abbreviating what i really want 2 say. limited by box on the screen. when will i say what i really mean?

people. relationships
April 2009 (age 25)

are so complicated. tainted when you refuse to keep them pure.
like lint in glass of water. can't see at first glance.

and there i was.

tangled in   his
sheets. drenched in   his
sweat while you send me sweet text messages wondering where
i'm at and why you miss me so much.

his touch don't carry the electricity it should like when you really
know somebody.

my fingers slide across his back
slip off 'cause they know he's not mine to keep
just a one-night thing
a fling
why do i allow myself to get flung

knowing there's someone special for me out there
someone waiting patiently

patiently while i pant, trying to fill my empty moments with kisses
and ripped off clothes. painting myself desirable in the shower
of his sweat. all this lust, on the very night of my good friend's
wedding where i bridesmaided and saw two people genuinely in
love and devoted to each other. six years of friendship, monogamy, and
celibacy. off to honeymoon and love each other the right way.

i see all this, this ultimate pure and strong relationship, and find myself
practicing the exact opposite. sleeping with a stranger. all the while there is
someone out there that truly knows and loves me.

and ain't this supposed to feel sweet? ain't our eyes supposed
to meet and shouldn't there be something beyond that glance,

something we share besides our bodies in the dark of the night.
beings colliding without thinking of consequences waiting with
the rising of the sun in two short hours.

i don't feel bad about this, just not good
not great
and i want to know what amazing feels like one day
but amazing is a combination between attraction and waiting
patience to build up love and desire
not a fire that can be blown out with one exhale

untitled
January 2010 (age 25)

sometimes
i wish
the moments would never end
wish i could travel back

nostalgia stings when you're in
grey sweatpants
and it's late
when life feels mundane

what happened to those tropical times
what became of the flutters from first kisses
of hands through hair
what can i give
to go back to
sunrise on beach
resting on your shoulder

i don't want you now
but i want
me in your arms
in that one space of time when i was yours
full of the hope for something
more

being a poet
doesn't help
only makes me relive each moment
more beautifully than the first time
make my heart ache at the art of it
make me yearn
to live those words
to be
eternal
in those moments

that made me feel
alive

sweet
misty
naïve

full of heartbeats

complete

hey beautiful wildchild.
i'm blessed to have shared part of my life with you.

please come say hello, and let's journey together.

@AliciaZakon

———————————

LAUNDRYANDLOVENOTES.com

THANK YOU

FAMILY: Mom: *for your consistent & intense love.* **Dad:** *though I highlight shortcomings in this book, I am not resentful. I love and appreciate you. Sisters* **Marlana & Carmela:** *for our laugh sessions & fond memories of pogo sticks, cracking knuckle contests, & sneaking tv through the reflection on the window. Nin-a-new much love nin-a-new.* **Aunt Casy & Uncle Richard:** *for your unwavering support & scrumptious food.* **Kaylene:** *for your never-ending enthusiasm for my art.* **Kyle & Keith:** *for all the smiles & wild dancing. My adorable nephew* **Josiah** *& niece* **Jade:** *for bringing such light & love to our family. Love & gratitude to my extended family:* **Big Ma, Uncle Will, Aunts, & Cousins Tiffany, Toshica & Darwit. _FRIENDS:_** *For holding me down. Special thanks to:* **Rashawne, Myette, PJ, Erica, Cherise, Anaiah, Tonesha, Nsa, John, Abeje, Jordan, Ariana, Kevin, Aida, Danielle, Latoya, Sharon, David F., Nina. _INSPIRATIONAL PEOPLE:_ Mama Naomi:** *for demonstrating how beauty & power coincide.* **Teri Goodman:** *for always going above & beyond in the way you guide, counsel, & love.* **Michael McBride:** *for your amazing vision.* **Marvin Goodman:** *for being an incredible student, colleague, & friend.* **Chinaka Hodge:** *for sparking my passion for poetry/spoken word.* **Linda Carr, Miriam Stahl, Victor Diaz, and AHA:** *for your support during my formative years as a teacher.* **_MY STUDENTS:_** *for your jubilance & for making my day on so many occasions.* **_UWI/BARBADOS FAM:_** *for the most soul-quenching 4 months of my life.* **_LA FAM:_** *you wildchildren have my heart!* **ORGANIZATIONS: Berkeley Boosters:** *Your program, along with countless Bay Area organizations serving low-income youth, nurtured my creativity & positively shaped my childhood.* **Youth Speaks & June Jordan's Poetry for the People:** *for molding me into a poet & speaker of truth.* **_WORK ON THIS PROJECT:_** *Thank you to anyone that helped me (in any way) on this project. Your support propelled me to finish strong. Special thanks to:* **Daniela Mejias, Adriel Luis, William Utley, Steven Turner, Tonesha Russell, Nijla Mu'min, Paul J. Griffith, Ise Lyfe, John Aymes,** *& my pre-release crew:* **Tiana, Imani, Keilani, Lena, Jayla.**

To the young angels in my life that passed too soon: **Anthony Lee Franklin, Heidi Lumbland,** *and* **Kwaku B. Agyapong Jr.,** *you will forever be with me.*

To people I didn't name: I trust you know how much I value your presence in my life. From picking me up for work, to treating me to lunch on campus, to letting me crash at your house when I'm in town, to listening to me vent about how I don't know to do with my life! What a blessing to have such a generous, loving support system.

KICKSTARTER THANK YOU'S

———

To everyone that made not only this book production possible, but also believed in the spirit of the *Laundry & Love Notes* Kickstarter project – THANK YOU. Your support is immeasurable.

Special thanks to these folks for your footwork, consultations, and continual words of encouragement. I couldn't have done it without you.

Casy & Richard Cann-Figel
Danielle Leslie
Obatala Mawusi
Jordan Warren
Aqueila Lewis
Marvin Goodman
Brenda M. Sanchez
Nancy Patel
Latoya Jackson
Abby Bobe'
Ariana Proehl
Ise Lyfe
Ruby Veridiano
Nsa Ntuk
Eric Freytag
Justin Martin
David Moody
William Correa
Aida Mariam
Jasolyn Harris
Ryan Nicole Austin
Jimmy - Nize Printing

& TeamZAKON!

ABOUT THE AUTHOR

Alicia Zakon made her mark on the poetry scene early. As a 4th grader, she won the Berkeley RESPECT Award for her poem "If There was Peace." With public accolades in her back pocket, she had the confidence to enter the Bay Area Youth Speaks slam scene in high school, quickly growing a following with her candid and colorful poetry.

Alicia began to hone her craft on the page and for stage as a Student Teacher Poet in UC Berkeley's acclaimed June Jordan's Poetry for the People class. After graduating, she served for three years as a performance arts teacher at her Alma Mater, Berkeley High School, working with upwards of 500 students in spoken word, drama, and her other passion, dance.

Alicia has shared her poetic artistry nationally and internationally—including the Youth Speaks Slam Finals in San Francisco, the Nuyorican Poets Café, the University of West Indies in Barbados, and Belize. Her written work has been published in several anthologies and her spoken word has been featured on various audio compilations, including the album "Spread the Word" by emcee Ise Lyfe. Alicia has also been a featured poet on NPR's All Things Considered radio broadcast.

Alicia currently lives in the San Francisco Bay Area where she is pursuing a lifelong dream of building a vibrant career as a writer and performing artist.

Visit Alicia at www.laundryandlovenotes.com. She loves meeting new people.